More Than a Sum of Diagnostic Differences:

A Positive Perspective on Autism and Asperger Syndrome

Laurel A. Falvo

More Than a Sum of Diagnostic Differences:

A Positive Perspective on Autism and Asperger Syndrome

ISBN 978-1450575751

First Printing: February 2010

Produced by Falvo Educational and Technical Services
for The Gray Center for Social Learning and Understanding
www.thegraycenter.org

Zeeland, Michigan

To Steve,
my partner, encourager, and friend,
and the most terrific husband
I could ever imagine;

To Ben, Nathan, and Jenae,
the most wonderful source of
laughter, learning, and love;

To God, who has given me this opportunity to use the
gifts with which He has blessed me;

And to the many people with autism who have inspired
me with your loyalty, determination, and
unique perspective on life;

Thank you!

TABLE OF CONTENTS

Chapter 1: What's Positive about Autism?

We are living in a world where the term *autism* is being widely used in the media and even in our daily conversations. All too often, it is accompanied by other words, tones, and facial expressions that indicate a sense of "doom and gloom." We are told that autism is a "thief" that "steals" children from their families, an "epidemic" desperate for a cure, and that autism is costing our society billions of dollars. There are often valid reasons for the stories, facts, and opinions that are shared. But what the news headlines, statistics, and campaigns frequently overlook is the positive side of the diagnosis.

The positive side of autism= People

This resource aims to put autism in perspective—*a positive perspective*—by focusing on an often neglected facet of autism...the people referred to by the diagnostic label, and those who love them, and who live, study, play, and work with them. Perhaps most importantly, it provides an opportunity to focus on what we are able to learn from those who bear a diagnosis of—or similarities to the strengths and challenges inherent with a diagnosis of—autism. Hopefully we can all find something to celebrate about these special people and the impact they have on our lives!

Chapter 2:
What is Autism?

Statistics, acronyms, and a hodge-podge of terms are used when describing *autism*. This neurological (or neuro-physical) disorder, or developmental disability, is often referred to as *ASD,* for *autism spectrum disorder.* Because the "umbrella" of the autism spectrum encompasses a wide range of delays, differences, or deviations, and even strengths, a wide variety of labels are used, including:

- *Classic* or *Kanner autism* (named after Leo Kanner, an Austrian psychiatrist), at the "lower-functioning" end of the spectrum;

Many terms are used to indicate a diagnosis on the autism spectrum

- *High-functioning autism, or HFA,* at the "higher" end of the spectrum;

- *Asperger Syndrome* (named after Austrian pediatrician Hans Asperger), also at the "higher-functioning" end of the spectrum;

- P*ervasive Developmental Disorder (PDD—* sometimes with an *NOS,* or *Not Otherwise Specified* accompanying it). PDD is often used synonymously with ASD; NOS typically indicates that not enough criteria were met for the individual to be definitively given one of the other labels;

- Less commonly, *Rett's Syndrome* and *Child Disintegrative Disorder.*

There is still much debate among researchers as to whether all of the above diagnoses are truly part of the autism spectrum, and/or whether other diagnoses, including *attention deficit disorder (ADD),* might also be part of the spectrum. Much of our understanding of the strengths and challenges of people with autism, and the strategies necessary for helping them achieve their full potential, is applicable across the entire spectrum. The specific diagnosis may not be as important as ensuring that we are aware of and responding effectively to the individual's unique needs, abilities, and other characteristics.

It can be misleading, and even detrimental, to use terms such as "low-functioning" and "high-functioning" when referring to any person, including someone with autism. Those who have limited verbal abilities are often referred to as "low-functioning." However, their restricted vocabulary may not be indicative of the potential complexity of their thoughts, dreams, abilities, and emotions. People with ASD may or may not have an IQ that is affected by the diagnosis. (IQ is "intelligence quotient," often used as a predictor of educational achievement or special needs). Although some may have a lower IQ, others may be judged as such because they respond differently to testing than we might expect. Others may have a normal to very high IQ (and may be referred to as high-functioning), but may have difficulty sharing what they know in an effective manner. If we judge that a person is low-functioning, we may rob him or her of

Terms such as "low-functioning" should be used carefully

important opportunities to learn new skills and achieve greater success, as well as depriving ourselves of valuable lessons that we could learn from that person. If we assume that a person is high-functioning because he or she is successful academically or has an impressive vocabulary, we may overlook significant needs for social supports or assistance with comprehension.

New statistics released in 2009 by the Department of Health and Human Services National Survey of Children's Health, using data from the Centers for Disease Control and Prevention (CDC), indicate that 1 in 91 American children are currently being diagnosed with ASD. This figure does not take into account the numerous adults living with autism, many of whom have been diagnosed late in life, perhaps after someone else in their family (a sibling, parent, or offspring) has been diagnosed. The statistics also, naturally, do not account for the countless individuals, of all ages, who have not yet been diagnosed, who have been misdiagnosed, or who may have traits similar to those on the autism spectrum, without a formal diagnosis.

Autism is diagnosed in both males and females. However, it is currently more prevalent in males, and may express itself somewhat differently in females. It is fortunate that several authors, including Temple Grandin, Liane Holliday Willey, Sondra Williams, Shana Nichols, and Lori Ernsperger have undertaken the important task of providing resources specific to the needs and unique expressions of ASD in girls and women, either from the perspective of a person with ASD, or from the perspective of a professional with many years of experience in learning from and assisting them.

The incidence of autism has been rising steadily. Just a few years previously, it was 1 in 160, and a couple of decades ago, 1 in 10,000. There are perhaps numerous reasons for the increase, including:

Autism statistics are rising steadily, likely related to a variety of factors

- We now have better methods for reporting and tracking diagnoses such as autism.
- Decades ago, our understanding of autism included only the "lower-

functioning" end of the spectrum. Now, many individuals with a normal to high IQ, who are perhaps more interested in social interaction (who might even be a spouse and/or parent and may be gainfully employed), are being included under the umbrella of an autism diagnosis. In other words, we are using a "bigger umbrella" than we were many years ago.

- Along with our increased understanding of autism is an awareness that the social differences seen in these individuals is not necessarily a choice. Instead, they learn and experience social situations differently than others, and benefit from additional instruction and support in order to achieve success.

- As more professionals are trained in identifying individuals on the autism spectrum, they are "catching" those who might otherwise have "fallen through the cracks."

- Genetics appear to play a role in passing autism within a family. As people with higher-functioning forms of autism (or some traits characteristic of the spectrum) are getting married and having children, often their children are also showing characteristics of the spectrum or eventually receiving a diagnosis of ASD.

- Along with the genetic rise in autism, environmental factors may also play a role in the increase (food, additives, vaccinations, viruses—many different things have been and will continue to be studied for a link to autism).

In other words, for a variety of reasons, there truly are more individuals with autism than there ever were before, increasing the likelihood that each of us will at one time or another be connected in some way with individuals with autism.

Research is leading us to believe there may be many sub-types and causes of autism

Much remains to be discovered about the exact nature and cause of ASD. It appears that researchers may eventually confirm that there are many different sub-types of autism, each linked to a unique cause, perhaps explaining why some interventions (such as a special diet avoiding certain foods) work well for some individuals, but not for others. It is also believed that some people may be born pre-disposed to developing autism, which is then triggered through something in the environment.

Autism can be more complicated when there are other diagnoses present

A diagnosis on the autism spectrum can be accompanied by other co-occurring (or "co-morbid") diagnoses, including (but not limited to) Down Syndrome, Obsessive Compulsive Disorder (OCD), Non-verbal Learning Disorder (NLD), Sensory Integration Disorder, Attention Deficit Disorder (ADD), and anxiety disorder or depression. This may make it difficult to get an accurate diagnosis, and may complicate the situation as parents and professionals work to assist these individuals in discovering and reaching their full potential.

Chapter 3:
Diagnostic Differences in Autism

While there is much about autism that is still unknown, there are certain accepted criteria being used to diagnose individuals as being on the autism spectrum. Each looks at differences, delays, and deviations present, usually from a very young age. A certain number of criteria need to be present, causing noticeable differences in learning and interacting, in order to lead to a diagnosis.

Unlike other diagnoses such as Down Syndrome, which is apparent through facial and other physical differences, or physical disabilities which confine a person to a wheelchair, autism is not typically associated with physical (appearance-related) distinctions which set a person apart from others. Instead, the responses of the person with autism to his or her environment are notably different, indicating a distinctive way of processing information and learning (or struggling to learn) from it. There are obvious social advantages to the lack of appearance-related distinctions in people with autism. However, this characteristic can cause others to have overly high expectations for a person's ability to interact with others, which can lead to misunderstanding, frustration, or even anger when the diagnostic differences of a person with autism contribute to difficulties in the interaction.

There are many wonderful books and other resources available to explain in detail what the diagnostic criteria are, and what they look like when present in young children, adolescents, and adults. The intent of this resource is simply to provide a basic understanding of how each area affects interactions between people with ASD and those who live, work, study, and play with them, as well as to examine the positive aspects of the people who bear a diagnosis of autism.

Language and Communication

Both expressive and receptive language skills can be affected by ASD

One characteristic which contributes to a diagnosis of ASD is the presence of delays or deviations in *language and communication*. Both expressive language (what is produced through speaking, writing, or even sign language) and receptive language (how language is processed when heard and read) may be affected.

Some individuals with ASD do not use verbal language to communicate, or have very limited words or signs to indicate their needs or thoughts. Sondra Williams, a woman with high-functioning autism, has shared that she was "non-verbal" or had very limited verbal ability until about the age of five. As an adult, she is re-examining the memories she has of her childhood (which are similar to video tapes in her mind), and is finally beginning to put words to the thoughts and feelings she was experiencing at that time. In other words, although she was not able to process those things or communicate them to others when she was young, she is now able to comprehend what was happening, and how she felt about it. Her phenomenal ability to share her experiences with the rest of us has been captured in her writing and poetry in the book, *Reflections of Self*, and her DVD, *Define Me*. Sondra and others have provided a vivid reminder that even when someone has limited verbal ability, they may have a wealth of ideas and information to share with the rest of us. It is fortunate that assisted communication, speech and language therapy, sign language, and other strategies are helping some individuals with ASD to connect with others in a way that had been previously unavailable to them.

Typically expressive language is a strength for people diagnosed with Asperger Syndrome. These individuals may sound like "little professors," even at a very young age, particularly if they are talking about an area of special interest. However, even though their expressive language may be very impressive, like those with other forms of autism, understanding language (comprehending what is read or heard), answering questions, and using language socially are typically a challenge for people with Asperger Syndrome.

Echolalia is frequently present in the language exhibited by individuals with ASD. They may parrot a word, phrase, question, comment, or lines from a movie they have heard previously, using this "script" to ask questions, give compliments, or simply seeming to "play" with language to entertain themselves. A parent asking, "Would you like a cookie?" may receive a response, "Would you like a cookie?" rather than the expected, "Yes" or "I would like a cookie." People with autism may use echolalia in appropriate contexts, or out of context, leading to confusion as others try to interact with them.

"Small talk" can be difficult for many people with ASD, both because of the fast pace and back-and-forth nature of it (requiring an ability to take turns), as well as the seemingly mundane topics such as weather, jobs, family members, etc., which may be outside a person's experience, interests, and comfort level.

People with ASD may require more processing time than others, contributing to difficulty experiencing social success. They may think of an answer to a question or information related to a current topic later than others, and by the time they are prepared to share their thoughts, the others in the interaction have moved on to another topic.

Effective communication involves more than just words

Much of our daily communication takes place outside of the actual words that are spoken or written. Instead, meaning is derived from context, tone of voice, body language, facial expressions, and even past experience (which provides opportunities for "inside jokes" between two people with shared experiences). People with ASD naturally gravitate toward the actual words that are spoken or written, and often miss the intended meaning because they have difficulty "reading" the other factors (noticing them, understanding their significance, and responding effectively). Their own attempts at using body language and facial expressions may be stilted or out of context, confusing communication rather than enhancing it.

Many people with ASD have difficulty making *eye contact*, or looking at another person's eyes during an interaction. Some are unable to use two senses at the same time. In other words, if they are listening to someone who is talking, they cannot also look at that person. If forced to look, they may no longer be able to listen. They may also be lacking an understanding of when and how to make eye contact, and of the important information that can be gleaned from it and communicated by it.

Interests and Imagination (or Behaviors)

> ***Restricted Repertoire* is a characteristic of ASD (seen in behaviors, interests, imagination, and need for routine)**

Autism is often associated with *stereotypical behaviors*, such as hand-flapping, rocking, or flicking fingers in front of the face. These behaviors are sometimes referred to as *stimming*—an often involuntary response of the individual with ASD to excitement or over-stimulation. For some, these responses fill a need; perhaps calming or reassuring them during times of stress or excitement, or providing additional stimulation when needed. Some individuals with ASD are aware of these responses, and have learned over time (or are learning) to replace them with a response that is less likely to draw attention to themselves, perhaps holding a "fidget" (or small squeezable or otherwise responsive toy or object), or sitting on their hands when they are around other people and sense a need to flap their hands.

Differences in imagination can adversely affect social interactions

Many people note differences in *imagination abilities* in people with ASD. It is not that they are completely lacking an imagination; rather, they may engage in more realistic imaginative play, or exhibit imaginative abilities within the realm of their special interests, or somehow be more restricted in their imagination. Where this becomes a significant issue in social interactions is when we recognize that we spend much of our daily lives engaging our imagination. We imagine what another person's response might be if we tell a particular joke or a favorite story, we imagine what might happen if we turn in an assignment a day late, or if we are unable to find our car keys. Many of our responses have first passed an internal "imagination test," where, through theory of mind (the ability to imagine what another person knows, thinks, feels, etc.) or other developmental strategies, we have imagined our own response and how others might respond to it before we do or say something. People with ASD are often missing valuable, relevant social information about themselves and others, and can be helped to interact more effectively through a variety of tools or strategies which provide additional details about what they and others could think, say, and do.

Another characteristic of ASD is *restricted interests*. Often people with ASD have a special interest that is unusual in its focus and intensity. It may be similar to the interests of one's peers, or vastly different. But this interest (sometimes referred to as a "perseveration") typically occupies the time, conversations, physical space, and emotional energies of the person with ASD. People with ASD are also known to adhere to strict routines and rituals.

The sum of differences in the area of behaviors, imagination, and interests can contribute to the often inaccurate perception that people with ASD are "in their own world," and lack an interest in connecting with other people. While some have little interest in social interactions, others have a strong desire to be included and accepted, but have difficulty achieving social success.

Social Participation

Another of the diagnostic criteria for ASD is a difference, delay, or deviation in *social participation*. The characteristics that are typically identified as being in the area of social participation include:

Social Participation is an area of difficulty inherent in a diagnosis of ASD

- Difficulty initiating and/or sustaining a social interaction (knowing what to say, when to say it, and how to hold other people's attention or maintain one's own attention to the interaction);

- Difficulty with turn-taking (reciprocal relationships), both in activities and conversations;

- Adherence to own rituals, rules, and routines;

- Difficulty noticing, understanding, or responding effectively to *unwritten social rules*; the expectations of others which govern so much of our daily interaction with them;

- Impaired emotional regulation, understanding of emotions in others, and ability to respond effectively;

- Difficulty with *Theory of Mind* (understanding that others have their own ideas, feelings, interests, etc. and using that information to guide interactions with others);

- Difficulty with peer to peer relationships (often individuals with ASD have an easier time interacting with people much younger or older than they are, especially during childhood and adolescence). This can naturally pose difficulties in a classroom consisting of children or adolescents who are grouped according to age.

Another common characteristic seen in individuals with ASD is the tendency to "meltdown" or shut down. A meltdown may exhibit itself as a tantrum, complete with screaming, falling on the floor, or yelling angry words. Shutting down may appear to others as the person "retreating to his or her own world," sitting in stony silence as life resumes around them. Typically these responses appear when the individual is overwhelmed by social or sensory input, rendering him or her unable to manage emotions and responses in a socially effective manner.

Sensory Integration

Sensory Integration Difficulties are common in people with ASD

Often individuals with ASD have difficulty with *sensory integration*. When a person's sensory system does not integrate (perceive, interpret, and respond to) sensory input (including sounds, tastes, textures, sights, smells, and other sensations) accurately or efficiently, he or she may:

- Have difficulty screening out unnecessary noises, struggle to focus on the important ones, and may sense some sounds as unusually painful;

- Have difficulty paying attention to important details without being distracted by tags in clothing, temperature, or other sensory input;

- Be intolerant of different textures when eating or touching things;

- Slam doors or use too much force in other areas, since the proprioceptive system (how the skin and joints work together) is not signaling how heavy the door is and how much force is needed;

- Walk into things or step on people's toes, due to a lack of understanding of where his/her body is in relation to other things or people;

- Be bothered by too much visual input—fluorescent lighting, too many objects or colors, too much activity or motion;

- Stand too close while talking with someone, or complain that someone else is too close, since he/she lacks an awareness of appropriate personal space;

- Use a voice that is too loud or too soft for the current social context;

- Shut down or melt down, when the sensory system becomes over-stressed.

Other Differences

Motor skills, both *fine* (such as writing and eating) and *gross* (such as climbing and running), may be delayed or different in individuals with ASD. While some may be gifted artistically, others may struggle with handwriting and other basic tasks. While some may be drawn toward playing sports, others may run, climb, or even walk in an awkward manner.

Many people with ASD have an enviable *memory* for facts and statistics. They may effortlessly memorize (and be able to recite accurately) dates, phone numbers, train schedules, or sports statistics. However, they may have significant difficulty with their "working memory" (or "practical memory"), which would enable them to remember where they put their shoes or when to turn in their math assignment.

Some people with ASD struggle to recognize people by their faces; a concept known as *face-blindness.* Whether this is due to their lack of eye contact (meaning that they seldom look at another person's eyes or face), a lack of understanding what to look for, or brain differences inherent in ASD, face-blindness can cause obvious difficulties in social interactions. Sondra Williams has indicated that she has frequently been embarrassed when she fails to recognize a close friend or even her own husband in public. She identifies people through their voice tones, shoes, and natural scents rather than their facial characteristics. While this has proven to be a mostly effective adaptive strategy for Sondra, it has obvious pitfalls, in that people may have different voice tones due to a respiratory ailment, and also frequently change shoes and/or colognes and perfumes.

Anxiety and depression are sometimes found in individuals with ASD, particularly as they near adolescence. There are some who believe this accompanies an increased awareness of their differences and of the difficulty of "fitting in" with the people around them.

Because each person with ASD is a unique individual, each person's diagnosis will also exhibit itself in a somewhat distinctive manner. However, the diagnostic criteria described above are used to identify a person's possible relationship to a diagnosis of ASD, which in turn can help determine what services or assistance the individual may need in order to reach his or her full potential.

This chapter has briefly described the differences typically found in people diagnosed with ASD. These differences, however, do not define them. They are part of who they are (part of that person's unique individual context, as described in *The Social Response Pyramid™)*, but each person is much more than the sum of his or her diagnostic differences!

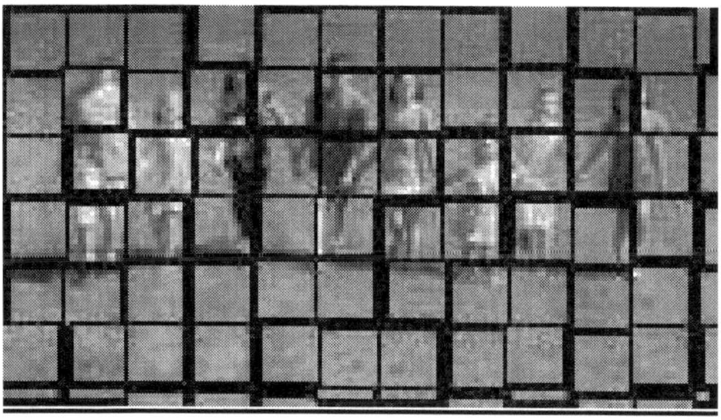

Chapter 4:
More Than a Sum of Diagnostic Differences

Who are you? How do you define yourself?

- What do you look like?

- How do you dress?

- How would you describe your personality? Are you shy or out-going? Intense or laid-back? Do you tend to see the positive side of things, or do you typically focus on the negatives?

- What interests you? Do you have hobbies that you like to engage in? Do you collect something? Do you read books about a particular topic?

- What are your talents? Are you good at something, either a talent that most people know about, or something obscure? What do you do well?

- What challenges do you face, either external or internal?

- How are your relationships?

- How well do you manage your emotions?

- Are you well-organized, or easily distracted from your goals and objectives?

- What are your hopes and dreams for the future?

- What do you fear?

- What expectations do you have for yourself, and for those around you?

Congratulations—you are a unique individual! No one is likely to have responded to the preceding questions in exactly the same way that you just did. Most likely, there is no one word that could adequately describe the complex and unique person that is uniquely "you."

In the same way, the word *autism* could never begin to sum up a person who carries this label. Each is first and foremost a person; a unique individual with hopes, dreams, fears, abilities, a distinctive personality, and challenges, just like anyone else!

All people—including those with ASD—are unique individuals

Often the diagnosis does not need to be used when referring to a person with autism. Each one is primarily a child, student, parent, or sibling, just like anyone else. When it is necessary to reference the diagnosis, those who are aware of the concept of "person-first language" deliberately refer to "people with autism" (or children, students, etc. with autism) with the label de-emphasized, being careful not to emphasize the diagnosis by putting it first, as in "autistic person."

However, there are also some people who have been personally diagnosed with a form of ASD who feel that "person-first language" devalues the positive and pervasive effect that autism has on them as unique

There are some who prefer to be referred to in a way that identifies them as being "on the spectrum"

individuals. They prefer to describe themselves as *autistics, auties, aspies, or aspergians.* Collectively they have made great strides in getting the rest of the world to hear, acknowledge, and learn from their experiences and perspectives.

Unfortunately, we live in a world where autism is not always perceived as positive, and where there is still much misunderstanding about the diagnosis. Circumventing person-first language and using the term "autistic child" can be misconstrued and misapplied to other diagnoses by people who are not sensitive to the nuances of these terms. In other words, we should not endeavor to set an example for people who might revert to using terms such as "Down Syndrome child," "diabetic child," or even, viewed negatively, "autistic child," losing the ground that has been gained in promoting their personhood before identifying the issues that they may face. We also cannot assume that everyone with ASD would choose to be known as an "autistic person."

We can show respect in the way we refer to a person with ASD

It is important for everyone to be sensitive to the different experiences, opinions, and preferences unique to each individual who has been diagnosed with a form of ASD. Applying this information can help us show respect in the way we refer to other people.

What About People Without ASD?

There are a variety of terms used to refer to people who do not display characteristics consistent with a diagnosis of ASD. Sometimes those people are referred to as "neuro-typicals," or neurologically typical, rather than displaying the differences inherent with ASD. Sometimes it is said (only half-jokingly) that those people are simply "not yet diagnosed" with ASD, given that often the more familiar we are with ASD, the more we begin to see similar characteristics in ourselves and others.

In fact, it is inaccurate to assume that only people ASD struggle with the types of differences detailed in the preceding chapter. Many people—who are not on the autism spectrum—struggle to be socially effective, or can otherwise identify with issues common to those with ASD.

It would be misleading and unwise to refer to anyone (either with or without autism) as "normal" or "not normal," since these terms have not yet been satisfactorily defined, and naturally are interpreted according to our own unique experiences and expectations.

Valuing each unique individual can lead to more successful interactions

Part of interacting successfully with others—with or without ASD—is understanding them and ourselves, and valuing and respecting both our similarities and our differences. We can acknowledge that a world consisting of clones, whether of ourselves or of anyone else, would likely be a boring and unsatisfying place. Our unique abilities, feelings, experiences, dreams, challenges, and expectations can be used to enrich our lives and provide valuable opportunities to learn and to grow!

Chapter 5: The Other People Affected by Autism

Most people around the world have been—or will someday be—affected in some way by ASD. Some live with a family member with autism. Some have a classmate or student who manifests the strengths and challenges characteristic of the diagnosis. Some people in the workplace have an employer, employee, or colleague who either is or appears to be "on the spectrum." Most of us interact at one time or another with people with ASD, whether in line at the grocery store, in the library, restaurant, or our place of worship, or as we travel around our community. Each of us is likely impacted in some way by a person or people with ASD.

Families

Families work to help each individual—and the family as a unit—to experience success

Perhaps no one has more experience learning from and loving individuals with ASD than their families. Parents, guardians, and siblings have daily and prolonged intimate exposure to the positives and negatives associated with the diagnosis. Theirs is an experience of hands-on learning as they not only become accustomed to the individual, but find ways to manage their intricate relationships on a daily basis. The common phrase, "Necessity is the mother of invention" takes on new meaning as the family struggles to find ways to communicate, manage emotions, organize possessions and daily tasks, teach and learn important concepts, and respond to meltdowns, all while forming their identity as both individuals and as a family unit.

Extended family members (including grandparents, cousins, aunts, and uncles) can be impacted by the diagnosis as they seek to understand how to interact effectively with a family member who exhibits unusual or unexpected responses to common family situations such as holiday gatherings. They may also be asked to provide *respite or support* for parents who feel they have nowhere else to turn.

Family members may experience grief...and may also be great advocates

It is not unusual for family members to experience various *stages of grief* as they come to terms with an uncertain future for their loved one, or accept that their own dreams may not come true for a son, daughter, sibling, parent, or grandchild. Their grief may at different times take on the form of shock and denial, pain and guilt, anger and bargaining, depression and loneliness, acceptance, and actively seeking solutions to their dilemmas. It is important for family members to accept that their loved one is a unique individual, and to identify the positives in their relationship (including their own and their loved one's abilities, dreams, feelings, etc.). Often family members become valuable advocates for one another. Family members should seek outside support as needed; either from friends or from professionals who can help them to achieve a healthy perspective, effective strategies, and much-needed encouragement and practical assistance.

School Communities

School employees can help individuals with ASD achieve success

Administrators trying to balance the budget and keep the peace might be reluctant to embrace a student who may require supports outside the regular classroom (or additional supports within the classroom), or who may present with behavioral challenges. It is important to recognize that not all students with ASD require additional supports, and not all cause disturbances during the school day. Administrators may be helped by getting to know the individual, finding what motivates him or her, and looking for ways to provide positive reinforcement as often as possible. Administrators are also important coaches for the rest of the school team; maintaining a positive attitude and willingness to work as a team with the student, parents, teachers, and support staff can go a long way toward ensuring a positive school experience for everyone.

Teachers can set a positive tone and promote success for everyone in the classroom

Teachers trying to manage the classroom and help each student achieve his or her own potential, often with little or no training specific to autism, and no extra assistance, might sometimes fear or resent the presence of a student who requires more intense daily support and instruction both in the classroom, as well as the lunchroom and playground. While it is time-consuming to be proactive in meeting the unique needs of a student with ASD, often potential problems can be averted by providing advanced instruction, visual cues, and information about what will be happening next. A teacher's sense of humor and positive responses to his or her students—including those with ASD—set an important tone of acceptance that goes a long way toward allowing everyone in the classroom to be successful both academically and socially.

Peers and classroom aides can be helped to respond effectively to classmates with ASD, which can increase everyone's success

Classmates may be afraid or irritated by the unusual or unexpected responses demonstrated by their peers with ASD. Sometimes they might take advantage of those differences by manipulating and intimidating those individuals, or bullying them. However, careful observation, and intentional support and instruction from the adults in the school environment can help other students to be supportive and understanding, and can foster valuable friendships between those with ASD and their peers. Several resources are available to help structure a safe environment for all students.

Parapros or educational assistants (sometimes referred to as "aides") are often employed as helpers for children with ASD in the classroom, lunchroom, and playground. They and their students are most likely to be successful when these helpers understand the differences inherent in ASD, work as teammates with the teacher, and find ways to enable their student to be successful with minimal intervention or re-teaching, helping them to look for and respond effectively to their teacher's and classmates' cues.

Therapists and Doctors

Therapists may provide a variety of specialized services to many individuals with ASD, helping them with their speech and comprehension, fine and gross motor skills, eating, recreational activities, and social interactions. Doctors, psychiatrists, and psychologists often tend to their physical (including diet, medication, and general health and well-being) and emotional health and well-being.

Workplaces

An understanding and supportive employer can assist a person with ASD in being successful in the workplace

Employers can provide much-needed exposure to opportunities for individuals with ASD to use their time and abilities to benefit others and to access an income to support their personal needs. An employer's willingness to provide additional instruction, feedback, and social understanding and supports can help an individual with ASD remain employed, while the workplace likely benefits from the individual's ability to work hard, to use valuable skills, and to be loyal to the place of employment. Persistence, flexibility, and acceptance can lead to a win-win situation for everyone!

An Important Role for Each of Us

As community members (neighbors, co-workers, childcare providers, etc.) going about our daily lives, we all are presented with opportunities to understand, support, encourage, and learn from individuals with ASD.

A variety of resources are available to help those living and working with people with ASD

Many great resources are available today to provide valuable information and support to those living with or caring for people with ASD, working in school environments, providing therapy, helping to decrease the incidence of bullying, and providing necessary life skills to those transitioning toward adulthood and independence. Some of those are listed at the end of this resource, or can be found by going to The Gray Center's web site at www.thegraycenter.org.

Chapter 6:
Independence vs. Interdependence

It is a popular goal; raising our children to the point where they are able to live *independently*. This term means different things to different people, but many are working hard to help their child with an autism spectrum disorder to achieve this goal.

While this may be a valuable goal, many tend to overlook one important truth: more than likely, none of us truly lives independently! A single mom may be raising three children, managing a household, making a living, and paying the bills all on her own. She may do her own driving, banking, minor home repairs, and shopping. Most people would agree that this is independent living. However, her situation may be more accurately described as living *interdependently* rather than *independently.* This is true when her mechanic maintains her vehicle, relatives or friends provide childcare when needed, another friend cuts her hair, and others advise her when she is facing difficult decisions. When she encounters electrical or plumbing problems in her home, she hires a professional to resolve these issues. She has a lawyer who guides her through legal issues, and a financial advisor who helps her set up and achieve financial goals. The fact is, she is successful not because she can do everything by herself, but because she knows where to go to get assistance for the things she cannot do on her own.

So perhaps our goal for our children (and even for ourselves) should not be independence, but *interdependence.* There is a continuum of interdependence, where some people will need greater levels of assistance than others. While some may need more assistance in the areas which require specialized training (i.e. legal and mechanical), others may need additional assistance in practical areas such as grocery shopping, meal preparation, paying bills, and transportation. It is important to teach as many of these skills as we can. Kids might help with cooking, cleaning, and laundry, and although they may not be old enough to drive, they can help navigate around town by choosing the next turn and explaining what to do when a detour is encountered. But we also need to be teaching our children how and where to access additional help when needed.

> ***Interdependence* is a worthy goal, achievable at varying levels for different people**

Various resources and strategies can help teens and adults identify (with help) where they may need assistance, and even guide them through some basic problem-solving so that they can increase their successful interdependence. Michelle Garcia Winner's *Strategies for Organization* (DVD) helps parents and professionals identify the organizational challenges which may be hindering a person's ability to be successful, and provides helpful suggestions and practical applications to assist them in asking for help, setting goals, and prioritizing the steps needed to bring them to completion.

Fostering Interdependence

We can help others gain skills for living interdependently

What are we doing to help those around us live successfully, at the level of interdependence that works best for them? We can start by looking at what we can do "with" them instead of "for" them.

- Are they eating and sleeping independently? What can we do to help them achieve these milestones, which are important for their self-esteem and future success in other environments?

- Do they have their own responsibilities, such as taking care of their own possessions, homework, hygiene, and timeliness for obligations? Are they aware of the expectations of others, and are we helping them to develop strategies for managing these responsibilities effectively, rather than stepping in and managing these things ourselves?

- Does someone need a job? We can sit with them and help them identify their abilities and interests, possible jobs and employers, and then help them develop a resume and a personal marketing strategy. (It may be helpful to have them job-shadow another person to ensure that they are knowledgeable about the skills and responsibilities inherent with a particular job, or to volunteer for awhile in a position that will give them valuable experience and exposure to people who could provide references). We can help them practice answering interview questions, and develop a plan for keeping a job (i.e. dressing appropriately, arriving on time, completing tasks accurately and completely, and clarifying responsibilities). Then provide encouragement and support--and possibly accountability--while they enact their proposed plan. Remember, parents do not need to do each of these steps themselves. In fact, sometimes it is better to have a mentor—relative, friend, community member, or social coach—helping an individual to set and achieve goals rather than a parent.

It is unfortunate that sometimes we tend to be too quick to decide what other people cannot do, without giving them an opportunity to try something. It is well-documented that people with ASD may need more exposure to opportunities to learn new skills than their peers, so patience is definitely a virtue for those who find themselves in the position of teaching life skills. But often, if given the opportunity, they will exceed our expectations for their ability to live interdependently!

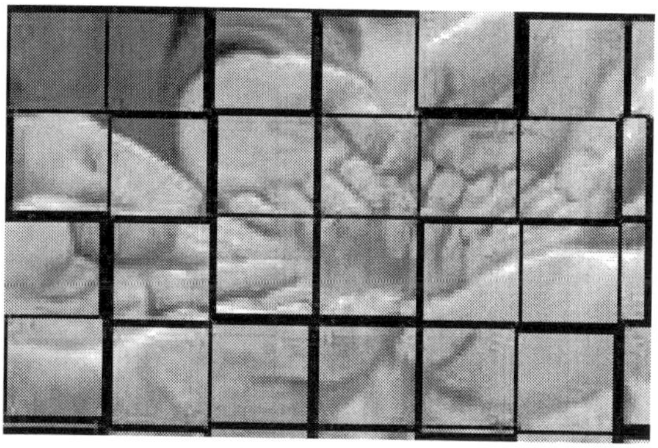

Chapter 7: Translating Diagnostic Differences into Mutual Success

Given the high incidence of autism, one thing is certain: almost every day and everywhere we go, we are likely to interact with one or more people affected by autism. Armed with an understanding of the diagnostic differences and a toolbox of valuable strategies, along with a desire to be socially effective, we can help ourselves and others achieve and enjoy social success.

Language Differences

Basically, *simple* language (which has just one meaning) is more likely to be a strength for individuals with ASD than *complex* or *dynamic* language (which has multiple interpretations or changes depending on the context). When we "say what we mean and mean what we say," (avoiding sarcasm and innuendo) we are communicating in a way that is more likely to be understood by people with ASD. We can also help by "using our words" to explain our thought process, and to clue them into the facial expressions, body language, and context clues that contribute to intended meaning as they participate in social interactions with others. Using visual cues, and providing plenty of "think time" to retrieve information stored in their memory can help people with ASD to be more successful in their interactions with others.

Avoiding assumptions and providing relevant instruction can help those with ASD

We can accommodate a person's difficulty with eye contact by asking him or her to clarify our instructions rather than insisting on eye contact when we are talking. We can teach that person to make eye contact as a way of establishing a connection with other people in the interaction, or to look for valuable information such as what we might be feeling or thinking. Various strategies, including role-play and analyzing videotaped interactions, may be helpful in developing meaningful eye contact.

Differences Noted as "Restricted Repertoire"

Regarding the "stimming" (or repetitive movements such as flicking fingers or flapping hands, rocking, etc.) of individuals with ASD, since these are generally "authentic responses" (stemming from what a person is thinking or feeling at that given moment), the individuals may not always be aware of them, and may not be able to anticipate or control them. Other people can help by being understanding and accommodating, by helping them find a time and place to engage in these responses, or helping to develop replacement responses as appropriate.

Special interests can be used for motivation and possible career success

Although the intense interests (or *perseverations)* common to ASD can make it difficult for parents and professionals to gain the attention of the person who would rather be talking or thinking about a favorite topic, these interests can also be used for motivation, rewards, and possibly even for a career path. This has been the case for Temple Grandin, author of several books including *The Way I See It* and *Developing Talents*, who has used her love for animals and her incredible ability to think in pictures to become very successful in designing humane livestock handling facilities! Often the rest of us have much to learn from the dedication, loyalty, and significant knowledge that a person with ASD may have acquired about a particular topic.

When a person lives in a world full of events and responses that appear random, as is often the case for people with ASD, it makes sense that they would grasp onto those things in life that are routine, predictable, and comfortable. Diagnostic differences that contribute to this sense of randomness and unpredictability include difficulty with *generalizing* and learning from experience, *executive functioning* (prioritizing, setting goals and following action plans, and being motivated), *theory of mind* (understanding that others have unique ideas, preferences, and more), *gestalt processing* (or an ability to "see the big picture"), *sensory integration*, etc. Schedules, routines, calendars, and clocks can all provide predictability and valuable reassurance for those who struggle to make sense of an otherwise seemingly chaotic environment. We can help by providing advanced notice when things are going to change, using visuals to help guide them through transitions (several can be found in *Visual Strategies for Improving Communication,* by Linda Hodgdon), providing calming strategies, and by recognizing when it might be better to ensure that a comfortable routine can be followed, at least for a time.

Comfortable routines can help individuals with ASD stay calm and experience success

Differences in Sensory Integration Abilities

You may or may not have a well-integrated sensory system. But either way, it is likely that you have developed strategies over the years to keep your system functioning more efficiently and to help yourself remain comfortable. Some people chew gum or drink coffee to stay alert. Some cross their legs while sitting and bounce their foot, or tap their pencil on a desk for additional input or to calm themselves. Some wear gloves when gardening because they do not like getting their hands dirty, or while cleaning because they prefer not to get their hands wet, or dislike the lingering smell of cleaning solution which might remain on their hands.

We may be able to provide valuable sensory strategies

When we are working with children, we have a tendency to remove such options which might improve their functioning or help them stay more comfortable. Often we do not allow chewing gum in class, we do not provide gloves for finger-painting, and we tell students to sit still while completing their assignments. Then we become surprised or frustrated when they have difficulty participating in the activity successfully. Occupational therapists have made great strides in introducing "sensory diets" in classrooms to provide the feedback so many students need, whether swinging, pushing or pulling heavy objects, "brushing" (the Wilbarger method), using weighted vests, bouncy seats or balls to sit on while working, etc. Strategies such as these can help students to be successful in spite of sensory differences.

It may be helpful to ask the individual with sensory integration dysfunction which sounds, smells, and other sensations are most disturbing to them, or take time to note their responses to various sensory stimuli. Sometimes we can change the environment to be more conducive to their needs, or provide strategies which would help them be successful in spite of their challenges.

When faced with a kindergarten student who attended well during whole-class activities, but stood frozen in the middle of the room when "free-time" arrived, one occupational therapist used sensory integration techniques to assist that student in successfully choosing and engaging in an activity along with the other students. Recognizing that "free-time" in a kindergarten classroom represents a somewhat chaotic environment with increased sensory stimuli, she addressed his sensory needs through quiet time and proprioceptive activities ("deep pressure" activities which helped to organize his brain and body), along

Success can be achieved by addressing underlying issues

with physical exercise. Taking a heavy instructional manual from the teacher's lounge, the occupational therapist instructed the teacher to have the student carry the manual to the school office anytime she noted that he was having difficulty selecting an activity. The teacher would say to the student, "Would you please carry this to the secretary? And while you're walking, think about what you want to do when you return to the classroom." The school secretary, who was aware of the situation, thanked the student, and sent him back to the classroom. By the time he returned to the classroom, he walked directly to a shelf and selected an activity (playing with cars or building blocks, coloring a picture, or reading a book). This strategy cost nothing, but was incredibly effective for both the student and the teacher, immediately decreasing frustration and increasing success! The key was that the adults in the environment recognized that the child was not being willfully disobedient, but due to sensory issues, was unable to comply until his underlying needs were addressed.

Differences in Social Participation

ASD is often referred to as a "social disability." Each of the diagnostic criteria has social implications. It is interesting to note that when a person with ASD is alone, the diagnostic characteristics are generally not a problem for him or her. It is primarily when other people, with their own expectations, experiences, feelings, etc. (or their individual contexts, as described in *The Social Response Pyramid™)* are interacting with people with ASD in a "social context" that the diagnostic differences cause difficulties for each person in the interaction.

For example, "stimming" (hand-flapping, rocking, flicking fingers in front of one's face) generally occurs when an individual is responding "authentically" to his or her own context. It typically is perceived by the individual as necessary and/or comforting. However, when the individual is in school with classmates, or in a crowded restaurant with other diners, suddenly that response does not work with the people around him or her, and the message is conveyed that he or she should stop, replace the response with something that works better with others, or go away for awhile.

To assist people with ASD in participating socially, we can provide mentors or peer supports, intentional, relevant instruction, and an extra measure of patience, understanding, and flexibility.

Putting it All Together

Those of us who comprise the "social context" can make it difficult –or easier-- for people with ASD to experience success

We cannot simply point to people with ASD as the cause of breakdowns in communication or other social interactions. The rest of us are both part of the problem, and part of the solution! We can continue to work at understanding ourselves and how we contribute (either positively or negatively) to an interaction, and help individuals with ASD do the same. Nick Dubin is the author of *Breaking Through Hidden Barriers* and *Diagnosis Aspergers: Nick Dubin's Journey of Self-Discovery* (a great DVD introduction to Asperger Syndrome) along with several other resources, and a young man with Asperger Syndrome. He once indicated that he is capable of feeling empathy, but on his own, does not always recognize what others are feeling in order to identify with them and respond effectively. He appreciates having people share their feelings with him, rather than making him guess the meaning of their facial expressions and body language.

Individuals with ASD can be interpreted as being "predictable in an unpredictable way." While we may anticipate that sensory input may affect them in unique ways, we may not know what will affect them from day to day, or how they will respond. While we may expect that they will exhibit social differences, they may catch us off guard by unexpected responses indicating a unique expectation or understanding. Their special interests, while unique in their intensity and focus, may change suddenly, or may remain the same for many years. As they gravitate toward the topics, objects, and routines which make them comfortable and bring them pleasure, we can learn more about their abilities, interests, and functioning level, enabling us to more adequately address both their strengths and their challenges.

> **Several strategies can help those with ASD to be more socially effective**

Several strategies can benefit individuals who are interested in becoming more socially effective, by helping them learn valuable information about themselves and others, and providing tools to help them interact more effectively with others. Carol Gray's *Social Stories™,* Michelle Winner's *Social Behavior Mapping™,* Kari Dunn Buron's *Incredible 5-Point Scale,* and Laurel Falvo's *Social Response Pyramid™* are among some of the strategies which can increase understanding and lead to effective responses.

Support groups can provide access to other individuals with similar strengths and challenges, along with facilitated social interaction and instruction. The Gray Center has a "Young Adult Network" to provide regular opportunities for young people and adults in West Michigan (generally ages 16-40) to meet for conversation and fun social outings.

Social Coaching is a personalized approach which provides on-going, one-on-one instruction and support as individuals set goals and action plans leading to successes, both great and small. The Gray Center is one of several businesses and organizations which provide this type of service, whether to provide immediate assistance with a particular issue, or to help clients look toward the future and develop and adhere to valuable plans for personal success.

Together we can celebrate success as we find ways to learn from each other and interact more effectively with one another!

Chapter 8:
Do We Need a Cure for Autism?

There have been many people over the years who claim to have "cured" someone with autism, or say that they themselves have been "cured." Talk of a cure is sure to spark heated debates as people feel very strongly either that a cure is necessary and should be the primary focus of research (and fundraising campaigns), or that a cure is not necessary and in fact devalues those living with the diagnosis.

Debate Surrounding the Search for a Cure

It is likely that the debate stems from the fact that the term *autism* encompasses such a wide range of abilities and disabilities, and touches the lives of millions of diverse individuals, each with his or her own perspectives, experiences, and expectations related to autism.

A "cure" for autism is a hotly-debated topic

There are some people who appear so deeply "locked within their autism" that a cure to uncover their seemingly hidden potential and enable them and their loved ones to enjoy a mutually satisfying relationship would be very welcome, indeed.

However, with all due respect to those who feel a need for a cure, others find that their personal experience with individuals diagnosed on the autism spectrum makes them uncomfortable with talk of a cure. Often both the distinctive abilities as well as the "quirks" associated with the diagnosis have combined with the individual's personality and life experiences to make them uniquely them. In other words, like the title of this book, they truly are "more than a sum of diagnostic differences!" Looking for a "cure" for something which is so intricately combined with the other aspects of who they are is practically tantamount to trying to cure a person's blondeness (or any hair or skin color), a persistent drive toward perfection, unusual and intense interests (which often end up benefiting our world in significant ways) or someone's creative view of life and/or artistic ability. Discussing the need to "cure" this aspect of their personhood implies that there is something inherently wrong with them that cannot be tolerated or lived with, much as we are trying to cure potentially fatal diseases such as cancer, heart disease, and muscular dystrophy.

People with ASD have made many contributions to our world

While people may have diverse opinions regarding the need for a cure for autism, hopefully we can all agree that people with ASD have provided numerous significant benefits to our world and perhaps to each of us personally. The following are some of the contributions that people with autism make to their families and to society:

Contributions in the areas of Language and Communication

As mentioned before, the sum of diagnostic criteria in the category of language and communication indicates that *dynamic language* is typically a challenge for individuals with ASD. This is language that is not *static,* but instead changes in meaning or intent over time, or within different social contexts. People with ASD tend to exhibit strengths in their ability to interpret language literally (or in a static manner). While this may confuse those of us who use context or prior experience to impose a variety of meanings on language, it can also be a source of delightful humor, provided that everyone is in on the joke. We may need to explain that there is no need to look for actual cats and dogs outside when it is raining very hard; instead, the saying "it's raining cats and dogs" originated many years ago when animals took refuge on thatched roofs to stay warm, and lost their perch when the intense rains came.

The *idiosyncratic* language skills of people with ASD (words and descriptions based on their own understanding and experiences) can provide new and unusual ways of understanding and appreciating our world. One example of idiosyncratic language would be an individual who refers to unplugging an electrical item as "plugging it out" (the opposite of "plugging it in"), which gives evidence to his or her literal interpretation of language.

Some individuals with ASD have an incredible ability to use language creativity to describe the world, along with their feelings and experiences. Sondra Williams is one such person, who shares her beautiful poetry and prose with readers in her book, *Reflections of Self.*

Contributions in the Area of Sensory Awareness

> **The heightened sensory awareness of individuals with ASD can greatly enrich our lives**

Given that many individuals with ASD are highly aware of sensory stimuli, they frequently provide others with an awareness of their surroundings that might otherwise have been missed. They often notice sounds, sights, and sensations that are easily overlooked by the other people around them.

Their caregivers, teachers, and peers may find their lives subtly or greatly enriched as they take time for shared experiences such as observing flowers growing along the side of the road, sounds of animals in the woods, a variety of sensations in different fabric textures, and more. Such sensory insights can significantly enrich our lives!

Contributions in the Area of Restricted Interests/Behaviors/Routines/Imagination

Our world has experienced and enjoyed many of the contributions of individuals with ASD in the area of restricted interests. Those intense interests, when channeled in ways that allow them to contribute to society, can provide personal employment and/or enjoyment to the individual, and sometimes great advances that benefit our communities and our world.

Temple Grandin is an example of someone who has used her love of animals and ability to think in pictures to advance our understanding and effectiveness in the area of livestock behaviors and humane slaughter. Other individuals have provided advances in our knowledge and experience with computers, the laws of physics, astronomy, archaeology, engineering, mathematics, politics, and more! In fact, it is speculated by many people that such famous historical figures as Ludwig van Beethoven, Wolfgang Amadeus Mozart, Vincent Van Gogh, Isaac Newton, Albert Einstein, and Lewis Carroll also displayed characteristics of the autism spectrum.

Contributions in the Area of Social Participation

Perhaps it is ironic that people with ASD, which is often referred to as a "social disability," have contributed so much to our society in the area of social participation! In fact, most people who are acquainted with an individual with ASD have had their lives enriched in one or more of the following ways:

People with ASD tend to be very loyal and dependable—characteristics which make for good friendships. They are often very genuine, or free from "social airs," having a quality of "what you see is what you get." Similarly, they take others at face value, frequently avoiding the social judgments, gossip, and distrust common to relationships among those who do not have ASD. Many people have been blessed with lifelong friendships with a person with ASD.

People with ASD tend to be very honest

People with ASD also tend to be very honest; a character trait that most of us value in close relationships. Questions will be answered in a genuine, frank manner, providing exactly the information that we were asking for. Of course, our expectations (or unwritten social rules) can be a stumbling block for those who excel in the area of honesty, when we ask a question hoping for a kind answer, receiving instead an honest but unfavorable response. This is not necessarily the fault of the person with ASD, but is instead our own shortcoming, as we find that we cannot manipulate the person with ASD into giving us the information we want, but instead are being given the gift of truth!

Additional Contributions

If we are honest with ourselves, most of us have had our lives positively impacted by individuals with

ASD. In addition to the contributions listed previously, most people eventually find that their experiences with ASD, while not always easy, have led them down a path that has exposed them to unexpected pleasures that they would not trade for anything!

The love, laughter, and learning that come from interacting with people with ASD are often a great blessing. So, too, are the other people that have come into our lives along the way. New friends (many of whom have had similar experiences), talented professionals, and sympathetic strangers all become part of the journey helping us to appreciate all that we have experienced, and encouraging us to keep going.

"Recovery" from Autism?

As an alternative to searching for a cure for autism, more recently, there has been talk and research surrounding the concept of "recovery" from autism. The dictionary defines recovery as "restoration or return to any former and better state or condition." At this time, there is no consensus on a definition of "recovery from autism." But given that the diagnosis of an autism spectrum disorder (ASD) is currently primarily anecdotal or based on symptoms, rather than a specific definitive medical or genetic test, the focus on recovery takes us away from the idea that a person needs to have autism removed, and instead, focuses on enabling them to achieve their full potential. Granted, the "norms" that we compare them to are still those of "neurotypical" peers (or those who do not have autism). Since autism still occurs less frequently than "neurotypical" does, we still use that standard of comparison.

There is still no consensus on a definition of "recovery" from autism

Generally, "recovery" from autism is referenced when the symptoms and characteristics which initially led to a diagnosis of ASD are no longer visible (or are not significant enough to draw attention or to negatively impact a person's ability to function alongside his or her peers). This may include a child's ability to be fully integrated into a regular classroom without outside supports, an average or above-average score on an IQ test and a test of adaptive functioning, and a lack of criteria (as defined in the "Diagnostic and Statistical Manual of Mental Disorders"— American Psychiatric Association) such that an autism expert (medical doctor or psychologist) could no longer give the individual a diagnosis of ASD.

Individuals who have "recovered" from autism have gained the necessary skills and understanding to function more effectively with others

There are certainly those who can attest to the potential for recovering from autism as defined above. Some children, after receiving more intensive therapies when they are young, move into middle school, high school, or college, without the need for outside supports. Many adults (who may be married and gainfully employed) who are just beginning to question whether they may have a form of ASD, may have in fact "recovered" from autism, even though they were never formally diagnosed when they were younger. (Diagnosing adults is complicated by the fact that research until now had primarily focused on the expression of ASD in children).

Has autism "gone away?" Given that there is a strong suspicion of genetic involvement in many cases of ASD, as well as possible accompanying biological and physiological factors, most likely the source of autism is still present. However, research continues to show that individuals are "recovering" through exposure to early intervention and a variety of educational, behavioral, and medical interventions. Although autism remains a part of who they are, we may conclude that individuals who have "recovered" from autism have gained the necessary skills and understanding to function more effectively with others.

The Important Role of Social Understanding

At this point, there is no "magic formula" for helping individuals recover from autism (or to function at a level consistent with that of their peers), or even to reach their fullest potential. Practical experience indicates that the answer is different for one individual than it is for another—and may vary even from one day to another. But social understanding plays an important role in the potential for successful outcomes for people with ASD!

Social understanding recognizes that "social" is a two-way street; interactions involve more than one person. Even when one has a "social disability," there is much that can be done to ensure effective, successful interactions.

The more that parents, siblings, grandparents, teachers and other professionals, peers, colleagues, spouses, and friends can assist individuals with ASD in gaining relevant social information and strategies for producing effective responses (combined with help meeting basic needs such as sensory integration, accommodating learning styles, help for depression, meeting medical needs, etc.), the more likely it is that everyone can maintain a positive perspective and experience and enjoy success!

A Note from Author Laurel Falvo

Dear Readers,

In the last several years, our understanding of autism spectrum disorders (ASD) has increased tremendously. Research and practical experience continue to help us recognize both the strengths and challenges of people with autism and Asperger Syndrome, and develop strategies to promote social understanding and effectiveness in our interactions with them. It is gratifying to see the wealth of resources on the market today, all of which provide beneficial "pieces of the puzzle" as we live, study, work, and play together.

It is my hope that this resource will provide valuable information, hope, encouragement, and support for your journey. This world needs more people who appreciate, respect, understand, teach, and befriend people with ASD! You may want to consider providing this resource to teachers, libraries, neighbors, and others in your community. Additional information is available through The Gray Center for Social Learning and Understanding at www.thegraycenter.org.

Now that you have finished reading or perusing this resource, it is your turn! I hope you will take a moment to complete both sides of the survey on the following page, and send it to The Gray Center. Your responses will assist us in producing new resources and educating (and encouraging) people around the world!

Best wishes as you continue to promote social understanding and social effectiveness in your corner of the world. Remember that even one person can make a huge difference in the lives of many people!

Laurel A. Falvo, CFLE
Certified Family Life Educator
Executive Director, The Gray Center
laurel@thegraycenter.org

About The Gray Center

The Gray Center for Social Learning and Understanding is a nonprofit 501(c)(3) organization dedicated to promoting social understanding between individuals with ASD and those who interact with them in the home, school, workplace, and community. Resources include a web site at www.thegraycenter.org, a bookstore and library, social coaching, presentations, a young adult network (in West Michigan), and more!

A Survey of Positive Perspectives on ASD

Please complete the following, and send it to The Gray Center at the address indicated below. Some responses (if permission is granted below) may be used in future resources or Gray Center promotional materials. Please neatly print or type your responses in the format (spelling, etc.) in which you would like it to appear.

Name:____

City: ____

Country: ____

Phone or email: ___________________________________

Your role with regard to a person with ASD (please check all that apply):

____ I am a person with ASD

____ I am a parent to a person with ASD (age of child____)

____ I am a sibling to a person with ASD (age of sibling__)

____ I am a teacher

____ I am a ______________________
(friend, neighbor, grandparent, doctor, etc.)

The Gray Center has my permission to include my responses (without my last name and contact information) in future resources and/or promotional materials.

Signed: ______________________________

(Do not sign if you would prefer not to have your information used in this manner).

Survey, Page 2

QUESTION: In your personal experience, what are some of the positives of autism and of people who have been diagnosed with autism? (Feel free to submit additional pages as needed).

Please send your responses (both sides along with any additional pages) to:

Laurel Falvo, The Gray Center
100 Pine Street
Suite 121
Zeeland, MI 49464

Or fax to: 616-748-6029

Related Resources:

The following books and DVDs (and hundreds of other great resources) are available at www.thegraycenter.org:

Laurel Falvo

ASD to Z: Basic Information, Support, and Hope for Individuals Diagnosed with Autism Spectrum Disorders

The Social Response Pyramid™ (DVD and Instructional KIT)

The Autistic Brain and the Neurotypical Brain: Bridging the Gap Toward Effective Social Interactions (workshop DVD)

Carol Gray

Writing Social Stories™ with Carol Gray (DVD)

My Social Stories™ Book

The New Social Story™ Book: 10th Anniversary Edition

Storymovies™ (DVD-Standard and professional editions)

Comic Strip Conversations

Gray's Guide to Grief and Loss

No Fishing Allowed

Michelle Garcia Winner

Social Thinking Across the Home and School Day (DVD)

Strategies for Organization (DVD)

Social Behavior Mapping (Book and DVD)

Growing Up Social (DVD)

Socially Curious and Curiously Social

You are a Social Detective

Superflex: A Super Hero Social Thinking Curriculum

Sondra Williams

Reflections of Self

Define Me (DVD)

Related Resources, continued

Nick Dubin
Breaking Through Hidden Barriers
Diagnosis Asperger's: Nick Dubin's Journey of Self-Discovery (DVD)

Kari Dunn Buron
The Incredible 5-Point Scale
A 5 is Against the Law: Boundaries Straight Up!

Catherine Faherty
Asperger Syndrome: What Does it Mean to Me?

Temple Grandin
Developing Talents: Careers for Individuals with Asperger Syndrome and HFA
The Way I See It: A Personal Look at Autism and Asperger's

Linda Hodgdon
Visual Strategies for Improving Communication
Solving Behavior Problems in Autism

Ellen S. Heller Korin
Asperger Syndrome: An Owner's Manual (I and II)

Barbara Newman
Helping Kids Include Kids with Disabilities
Autism and Your Church

Another great resource: ***The Planner Guide,*** available at www.theplannerguide.com

About the Author:

Laurel Falvo, CFLE, is a Certified Family Life Educator who lives in Holland, Michigan with her husband and three children. She graduated from Calvin College with a degree in elementary and bilingual education.

Through her work as the Executive Director of The Gray Center for Social Learning and Understanding, Laurel has been privileged to interact with and learn from a variety of people, including those with ASD and their families.

Laurel frequently provides training to teachers and other professionals, as well as to friends and families interested in learning new strategies to interact more effectively with others, including people with autism spectrum disorders. Laurel also provides social coaching and consulting services for adults, teens, and children.

Laurel is the author of *ASD to Z: Basic Information, Support, and Hope to Individuals Diagnosed with Autism Spectrum Disorders,* and various resources enabling parents and professionals to use her educational tool, *The Social Response Pyramid™.* She writes a weekly email article, *The SUN News,* promoting social understanding and autism awareness.

Laurel and her husband Steve have produced this resource through Falvo Educational and Technical Services, on behalf of The Gray Center for Social Learning and Understanding. Special thanks to Amy Monteith and Jill Monteith, Marcia Hill, and Karla McGee for their help with editing and providing feedback on this resource.

More Resources by Laurel Falvo

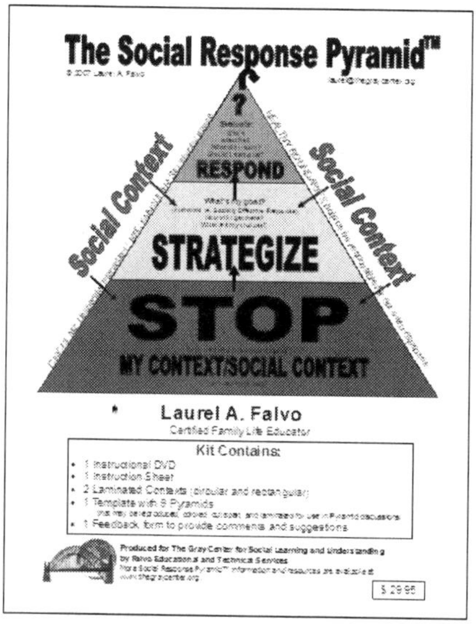

The Social Response Pyramid(TM), an educational tool developed by Laurel Falvo, is a visual representation of social understanding and social effectiveness--how we can better understand ourselves and others (including people with autism spectrum disorders) in order to develop and utilize strategies to increase the effectiveness of our responses. It can be used by anyone and for anyone! *The Social Response Pyramid Instructional KIT* contains all the pieces needed to have your own "Pyramid discussions," and an instructional DVD with video clips of Laurel using this resource with her own family to teach concepts such as "fitting in," mealtime manners, resolving conflict, etc. This *Instructional Kit* is available for purchase along with all of Laurel's other resources at www.thegraycenter.org.

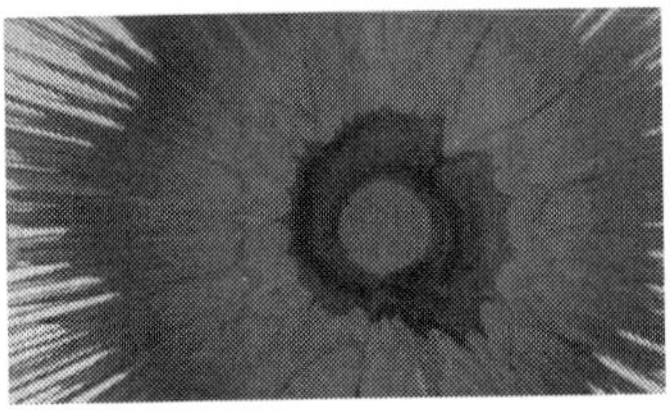

The SUN News is a weekly email article written by Laurel Falvo to increase autism awareness and promote social effectiveness. People can subscribe to this free resource at www.thegraycenter.org, and read past issues on Laurel's blog at http://graycenter.wordpress.com.

Social Coaching and Consulting

Laurel has combined her years of experience at The Gray Center and as a parent, along with her training as an elementary teacher and Certified Family Life Educator, to provide **Social Coaching and Consulting** services. Parents, teachers, young adults, and children use her services to identify goals and develop strategies for improving their lives and enjoying social effectiveness. More information is available at www.thegraycenter.org.

COMING SOON...a new DVD resource by Stephen and Laurel Falvo:

Why Do They Do That?

Information and Suggestions for Kids, Teens, and Others Who Have Questions About Autism and Asperger Syndrome

Go to www.thegraycenter.org for more information.

6825416R0

Made in the USA
Lexington, KY
23 September 2010